A SPIRIT DAUGHTER
WORKBOOK

WRITTEN BY
JILL WINTERSTEEN

FOR VIRGO SEASON
AUGUST 23RD- SEPTEMBER 22ND

THE NEW MOON
THURSDAY, SEPTEMBER 14TH
6:39PM PT

PGS. 2-15: VIRGO SEASON
PGS. 16-25: VIRGO NEW MOON
PGS. 26-27: VIRGO SIGN INFO
PGS. 28-31: ASTROLOGY FORECAST

VIRGO SEASON

From the fires of Leo Season, we meet the grounded energy of Virgo. Ruled by Earth, Virgo Season ushers in a period of transition as we move from summer to fall and feel our energy settle and refine. This period gives us a foundation to rest upon as we process the events of the past and future. It allows us to organize our lives after the chaotic burst of energy Leo Season often brings. The past four weeks gave us time to define and feel who we really are in this world. Virgo Season brings us an opportunity to show up as that person and realize our inherent self-worth. It is a time to let go of self-doubt, perfectionism, and self-criticism as we step into our potential in this lifetime. Virgo's energy helps us embrace our authentic self realized in Leo Season while accepting it with compassion, forgiveness, and strength.

It does not matter whether you have Virgo predominantly in your chart or not. Virgo Season helps everyone see their potential. This season shows us who we could be if we allow ourselves to fully step into our power. It is also a time to find balance between who we could become and who we are right now. Virgo reminds us that if we are always comparing ourselves to our ideal version, then we will never experience true joy. On the other hand, if we stop growing and striving to become a better version of ourselves, then we stagnate and become unhappy, or worse. We must find balance between accepting ourselves as is and wanting to transform into the next version of ourselves. The question of the season becomes: How can you love and accept yourself today while working to become your future self?

The first step in accepting yourself as you are today is letting go of conditions you must meet for love and acceptance. We often hold ourselves to an impossible standard, and when we fail to meet it, we fall prey to shame, embarrassment, self-doubt, and should-ing ourselves. We tend to hide our mistakes and mull them over, forgetting that others love us and want to support us. We feel that we are the only ones going through something and that everyone else has their life together far

VIRGO SEASON

better than we do. We also compare ourselves to others without even knowing them or understanding their struggles. We often tell ourselves that we have to meet certain criteria to be loved by others or to love ourselves. We may even judge our worth on what we do, not who we are.

As we journey through Virgo Season, become aware of the conditions you place on yourself for love and acceptance. What impossible level of perfectionism are you holding yourself to and why? We often feel that we have to be perfect to receive love and be worthy. Over this season, began to teach yourself that you are worthy of love, acceptance, and fulfilled dreams just as you are right now. You do not have to do anything more than what you are doing right now. Begin by embracing all aspects of yourself this season. Purge your consciousness of unworthiness at the beginning of Virgo Season by making a list of all the reasons why you don't believe you deserve love, belonging, acceptance, or fulfilled dreams. Write unrestricted and break free of the bonds of shame that keep you tied to a life of self-doubt. What don't you feel you are good enough for? What in your past or present is preventing you from owning your magic and declaring your worth to the Universe?

Letting go of these things that make you feel unworthy can be a long process. Allow this season to start you on the road of accepting your worth and cultivating a life that is full of everything you deserve. You deserve love, you deserve joy, and you deserve to have in your life people who accept you for who you are today. These are not things you need to jump through hoops for. Rather, they are your birthright as a human. You may have been taught differently growing up, and perhaps you were given conditions that you had to meet to earn love and acceptance. But that is not the way you have to live. It may take work to get there, but you can heal yourself and realize that your self-worth as a person does not depend on anything other than you being yourself. It all starts with a deep self-acceptance and appreciation despite any experiences that may have caused you to feel pain, shame, or unworthiness. What do you need to heal this Virgo Season to begin to feel your worth and know you are good enough?

Healing is at the heart of Virgo's energy. This season is a time to heal the places in you that feel unloved. It's a time to write yourself love letters about all the wonderful gifts you have to give the world, and a time to have compassion for yourself. It's also a time to define your boundaries both with yourself and others. Healing is often inked to boundaries. You must be willing to say yes to the things that matter and no—without guilt—to the things that feed your insecurity or sense of scarcity. Some of the boundaries will be with yourself, including your thoughts and your habits. Others will be with friends, colleagues, and other partners. Align with the Earth element this season to feel where you need boundaries, then know you are worthy of upholding them. You are worthy of the healing that strong boundaries provide.

Many of the boundaries created in Virgo Season can help you carve out time to work on yourself, your healing, and your worth. When you have a set time to work on yourself each day, it becomes easier to find balance between who you are and who you could be. You can accept yourself as you are while knowing you have time and space to become your next version. Over this season, align with the organizational energy of Virgo to create a schedule or routine of healing and growth. This may look like taking a class or reading a new book. It may be making time to meditate or journal each morning. It might be weekly acupuncture or yoga classes, or some other healing modality that serves you. The key is to give yourself permission and time to evolve while knowing you are still worthy of everything you desire right now. Work on yourself because you can and because it's enjoyable to grow, not because it's required for you to be good enough. You're already good enough.

HOROSCOPES

ARIES RISING: This season and New Moon affect your Sixth House of Service. It is a time for you to evaluate how you are giving your gifts, including your fire, to the collective. It's also a time to contemplate what is holding you back from contributing your talents to something higher than yourself. You often have brilliant ideas that come in flashes of inspiration. They fuel you for a bit, and then they quickly fade away. Over this season, look for rituals and practices that allow you to sustain your efforts and motivation. What are you ready to commit to over the long term? What gifts deserve your full attention and motivation? And how can you create a pace of life that is sustainable for your energy?

TAURUS RISING: This season and Mew Moon affect your Fifth House of Creativity. It's a time for you to embrace creative endeavors with patience and commitment. It's also a time for you to recognize that a new portal of creation is calling you, but you are resisting it. Creative work often asks us to leave our comfort zones. While this can feel scary, it's one of the avenues for true innovation. Create rituals that ground your energy and connect you with your inner resilience this season. From this stable platform, allow yourself to express your creativity in new forms. Be receptive to downloads for creative intuition coming your way, and know that you are ready for all of them. What new creative work is calling you? Are you answering the call? If no, then why not?

GEMINI RISING: This season and New Moon affect your Fourth House of Home and Family. Virgo in this house adds organization to your home. This may manifest as a neat and tidy closet, or it may cause you to become the person who manages family and intimate relationships. You may find yourself mediating others' debates or relationships throughout your life, and this season is no different. When you are asked to oversee family affairs, use your intuition and know you carry the power to mend hearts, minds, and souls. Be sure to replenish your own spirit though. Taking care of others, especially those close to you, can be exhausting. While you may enjoy it and be good at it, still take time this season to give back to yourself.

CANCER RISING: This season and New Moon affects your Third House of Communication. It's a time to lean into your intuition and be open to messages coming to you. It's also a time to ask yourself if you are blocking your intuition out of fear, overuse of logic, or mistrust. As you navigate this season, let your intuition lead the way. Create practices and rituals that allow you to connect deeply with your body and settle your nervous system. This strong foundation will provide a pathway for your intuition. Be open to receiving it and, most importantly, following it. Over this season, practice, letting it lead you. Resist the urge to question it or ask for proof. Instead, follow your inner knowing to build trust in yourself. What does your intuition feel like?

LEO RISING: This season and New Moon affect your Second House of Resources. With Virgo here, you are well organized with your finances, possessions, and resources—or at least you have the potential to be. Over this season, look at how you are managing and relating to your energetic resources. Create practices that help ground and settle your energy while replenishing you. As a Leo rising, you tend to spend a lot of energy outward. It's time to reclaim some of those vibrations and restore your spirit. Throughout Virgo Season, be a little quieter than usual. Conserve your energy and observe how you feel, not spending it so freely.

HOROSCOPES

VIRGO RISING: This season and New Moon affect your First House of Identity. It's a time to define how you want to be seen and how you are showing up in the world. With Virgo in this house, your identity can take on many forms. You may be a healer, an intuitive, an organizer, or a mentor. Ask yourself which vibration of Virgo you most identify with. Also, ask yourself if people are seeing you as one of these archetypes. How do you want to be seen? Then look at what energy you are projecting into the collective, and ask yourself why. Over this season, create practices that help you feel your truth and the energy you want to emit. Spend time each day journaling and creating "I am" statements that resonate with you. Feel into who you are and who you want to be.

LIBRA RISING: This season and New Moon affect your Twelfth House of Spirituality. This is a wonderful time to dive into your spiritual practices and make them a habit. You thrive with daily routines of meditation, journaling, yoga, and other methods of mindfulness. You often get into great routines but then lose focus when something throws you off course, like vacation, a great relationship, or even just summer. Now is the time to carve out how you want to connect with your spiritual growth. What practices are calling you? Can you commit time each day to them and yourself? You will find you are calmer, at ease, and present when you ground your energy and stay rooted in your spiritual path.

SCORPIO RISING: This season and New Moon affect your Eleventh House of Community. This is a time for you to align with your community and people with whom you have a true sense of belonging. These people may or may not be your family or people you grew up with, and they may not even be close friends. These are the people you share ideas with and who align with your core beliefs. They are the people you want to hold rituals or Moon circles with and bring together to share in an experience. Magic is always a big part of your life, and so is power. Over this season, build routines that allow you to connect with your power and your willingness to understand the depths of your psyche. Then look around to see who can share this often solo adventure with you.

SAGITTARIUS RISING: This season and New Moon affect your Tenth House of Career. This is a time for you to contemplate your life's work. Not just your job or the thing you do for a paycheck each week, but the work you are here to accomplish. Set aside time each day to do something that gets you in touch with the great work calling your soul. You can try journaling each day about five things you want to do or experience in your life, then see what patterns emerge. If you have an idea of the work you want to commit to, spend time making plans or carving out steps that will move you forward on your path. Also, notice if you have any hesitation around committing to something, and ask yourself why. Is there something you are afraid of losing if you commit to your work?

CAPRICORN RISING: This season and New Moon affect your Ninth House of Knowledge. This season is a time for you to widen your perspective and experience something larger than yourself. Learn something new, plan a trip, have encounters with different cultures, or just shake things up in your world a bit. It's also a time to lead with your intuition and allow it to take you to new lands. Let your spirit wander a bit, and know that not everything in your life needs to be planned. Let go of well thought-out itineraries this season and instead wing it. Let your inner compass steer you near and far. Get lost and find your soul, have an adventure without knowing the outcome, and trust life a bit more than usual this season.

HOROSCOPES

AQUARIUS RISING: This season and New Moon affect your Eighth House of Personal Growth. It's a time to go within and process emotions or energy in need of attention. Ground your vibration through daily practices that allow you to access your soul on another level. This season is an opportunity for you to evolve and even rebirth yourself. What is ready to begin again within you, and what is ready to end? Contemplate the cycles of your life and energy this season and feel what is waiting to expand you into the next version of yourself.

PISCES RISING: This season and New Moon affect your Seventh House of Relationships. It's a time to put some attention and intention into your partnerships. Which ones are serving you? And which ones need a shift? This season is also an opportunity to look at whether you do or don't add the energy of perfection into your relationships. Notice if you expect relationships to be perfect or if you are accepting of their natural imperfection. Also, be aware of how you may be holding yourself to impossible standards in a relationship or if you are doing this to someone else. Relationships are dynamic. They do not exist in a bubble. They are affected by many things and will never be perfect or even predictable. Become aware of your expectations this season regarding partnerships and ask if they are valid.

TIPS FOR VIRGO SEASON

8 TIPS FOR OVERCOMING PERFECTIONISM

SET THE TONE OF YOUR LIFE WITH THE RITUALS YOU DO EVERY MORNING

TELL YOURSELF THAT YOU ARE GOOD ENOUGH EVERY DAY

DECLUTTER YOUR SPACE, YOUR MIND, AND YOUR HEART

HAVE FUN WITH BEING IMPERFECT

REMEMBER THAT YOU ARE ALWAYS IN CONTROL OF YOUR REALITY

1. BEGIN

There is no perfect time to start something. When taking on new projects or new ways of being, we first must just begin. Often this is scary, as we feel the starting point is arbitrary. But actually, when we simply start something, without overanalyzing its timing, we flow directly from our intuition. We essentially do start at the perfect time; it's just not definable. Our instinct takes over and gives us the drive and motivation to begin. When we stop analyzing and worrying about the perfect moment, we unlock the part of us that instinctively knows the ideal time to begin. So don't over think it. When your gut tells you to start, then it's time.

2. CELEBRATE EVERY VICTORY

Life does not have to be perfect to be wonderful or celebrated. As you move through your journey, celebrate every victory, no matter how small. Perfectionism can often make us feel dissatisfied with what we have accomplished. We think it is never good enough, and we miss an opportunity to celebrate how far we've come. Take the time to acknowledge what you have accomplished each step of the way. Pat yourself on the back and thank yourself for what you've completed.

3. DON'T SWEAT THE SMALL STUFF

See the bigger picture of your life and recognize that not all pieces need to be perfect for the puzzle to be beautiful. We often get caught in a trap of details that don't matter in the grand scheme of things. We overanalyze and nitpick as a way to fulfill our need for perfection, but in reality, we are wasting our precious energy. Yes, many things matter, but many other things don't. Learn to discern where to place your focus, and avoid spending time on the intricacies that don't contribute to the bigger picture.

8 TIPS FOR OVERCOMING PERFECTIONISM

4. EMBRACE FAILURES

Failures are powerful opportunities for growth and learning. Everyone fails at some point and are better off for the experience. The importance of failure lies in the lessons it teaches us. Instead of shaming or blaming yourself, try to view the failure as a positive event and extract the knowledge it provides. Failures show us information about ourselves. They teach us about pieces we haven't thought about before, and they shed light on how to work with the unknown. Failures ultimately give us a more in-depth understanding of ourselves, our project, and our energy. Learn to embrace failures and allow them to open doors into places you would not have reached otherwise.

5. ACCEPT THE PAST

Fear of regret is one of the most significant pieces of perfectionism. We become so afraid of making a mistake and feeling regret that we fail to try anything at all. Often this fear is a result of a past mistake and the subsequent emotions that occurred afterward. We falsely believe that if we are perfect this time around, we won't have to feel regret. Learn to accept that everything unfolds at the right time in the right way, and sometimes this does not match our expectations. When our expectations are not met, we may feel we did something wrong. Trust that life is flowing in the best way possible, even if it appears to be not working in your favor. Accept the events of the past and don't allow them to hold you back from your future.

6. BALANCE WORK AND LIFE

The more we work, the more time we give ourselves for perfectionism. Schedule time for play, nourishment, and life outside work. Even if you initially resent taking time away from your work, the break will provide a new perspective and will help you not obsess over every detail. Don't let the pendulum swing the other way either, though, by depriving yourself of the time and effort you need to work on yourself or your projects. Find a balance between work and play. This balance will help you maintain a healthy relationship with yourself.

7. AVOID COMPARISON

Comparison is a road to nowhere. We can never compare ourselves to others because we are all unique snowflakes with our own life paths and energetic evolution. Comparison can fuel perfectionism because it creates an unobtainable goal. It makes us feel that we are not good enough because we can never be someone else. Learn to love yourself and your unique path. Find gratitude for your journey. Allow this love and gratitude to bring the focus back to yourself and your goals.

8. ACCEPT YOUR BEST + ASK FOR HELP

Always try your best, but also accept your best. Most things in life don't need to be perfect. If they do require perfection, get help so that you are pulling together everyone's best attributes for the project. None of us are perfect alone, and it is futile to try. But together we can make something beautiful.

CRYSTALS FOR VIRGO

SMOKEY QUARTZ is a wonderful stone for grounding and releasing negativity. It will help you rid yourself of unwanted feelings, including anxiety and perfectionism. Hold it when you feel your mind begin to criticize and critique, as these are the lower vibrations of Virgo Season. Have a piece near you while you meditate to ground your energy and help you feel connected to the Earth. It will stabilize and strengthen your energetic field while sending any lower frequencies back to the Earth to be recycled.

Smokey Quartz vibrates to the mantra: "I am grounded."

DUMORTIERITE brings both patience and the will to stand your ground. Its vibration centers your energy and clarifies your vision. It helps you understand who you are and how to take control of your life by believing in yourself. It also helps you access your psychic visions and intuition. Hold a piece when you feel confused or overwhelmed by information and need to access your inner knowledge to make a decision. If the external world is drawing too much of your attention, place a piece in your pocket to stay grounded and centered on yourself.

Dumortierite vibrates to the mantra: "I am clear."

PINK CALCITE is a stone of self-love and self-acceptance. It will assist you in loving every part of yourself and feeling your inherent worth. It also helps direct energy away from negative vibrations of fear, anxiety, and nervousness that can come with the low side of Virgo's energy. It is a wonderful stone if you need to return to your inner home to raise your self-worth and trust in yourself. Hold a piece while meditating when you need to let go of self-criticism and heal yourself with love.

Pink Calcite vibrates to the mantra: "I accept myself."

AMAZONITE helps you speak with truth, clarity, and heart. It calms any anxious feelings and centers your energy, allowing hope to flood into your energetic field. It's excellent to meditate with when you feel stressed by choices, decisions, or an overabundance of information. It's also an excellent stone for manifestation. Keep some near you when envisioning how you want your life to unfold. It helps keep you calm while transitioning to a new life and keeps you focused on the best possible scenario. Have some near you when creating plans, taking action, or shifting phases of your life.

Amazonite vibrates to the mantra: "I am calm."

UNAKITE brings you in touch with your psychic visions and intuition. It can even bring them to you while you sleep by calming any anxious vibrations that come up in the night. Place a piece under your pillow so you have a calming night's sleep and awaken with a knowledge of the future. It can also help clear attachments to old habits and ways of thinking or being. If you feel something is holding you back from pursuing your dreams with full commitment, look to this stone to free you. Hold some while meditating to help move your energy forward in a new direction, guided by your intuition.

Unakite vibrates to the mantra: "I see."

VIRGO MEDITATION

EARTHING + WALKING MEDITATION

Earthing is a practice of connecting with the Earth and harnessing its frequency to balance your energy. We have become disconnected from the Earth due to shoes, the homes we live in, and the cars we drive. For centuries humans walked barefoot on the Earth, and our energetic bodies still crave this connection for restoration and balance. Over Virgo Season and on her New Moon, find an area in nature where you feel comfortable walking around in bare feet. Allow the Earth's energy to bring harmony to your system and ground your vibration, leaving you restored and clear minded.

Earthing is a simple technique. Find an area where you can safely connect with the Earth, then take off your shoes. Before beginning, firmly press the Kidney One acupuncture point. Find this point on the sole of your foot, about a third of the way down from your second toe. When activated through pressure or acupuncture, this point connects us to the infinite energy of the Earth. It also grounds our energy, restoring balance to our system. Press this point on each foot for about fifteen seconds. Then place your feet on the ground, observing the sensation of your bare feet on the Earth. Feel the texture of the Earth as you wiggle your toes in the soil or sand. Feel the temperature of the Earth and even her density as you allow yourself to sink in and be supported by Mother Nature.

Close your eyes to bring even more focus to the sensations in your feet. Clear your mind and focus on your breath as you continue to connect your feet to the Earth. Allow your breath to help anchor and steady your mind. Say to yourself, "I am inhaling" as you inhale, and "I am exhaling" as you exhale. Feel the Earth's energy drawing up through the Kidney One point on each inhale, like roots drawing up water. Then feel your connection with the ground strengthening on each exhale. You may even feel the surface of your feet expand on each exhale, helping enhance your connection.

Keeping your eyes closed, add some movement to your body. Slowly shift your weight to your right foot as you inhale, then pause for the exhale. Shift your weight to your left foot on the inhale, pausing here for the exhale. Continue playing with your weight for about 10 breaths, then stand still with both feet firmly on the ground. Open your eyes while staying deeply aware of your feet and the ground beneath you.

Begin to walk on the Earth slowly. You can have a designated path, or you can walk freely. Continue to be mindful of your breath as you walk, inhaling as you lift your foot and exhaling as you place it down. On each exhale, allow your full weight to land on the ground, feeling the Earth supporting you. As you lift each foot, still feel the opposite foot's connection on the ground, maintaining your relationship with the Earth. Continue walking like this for 10 to 15 minutes. Make your movements slow and purposeful, as if you were learning how to walk for the first time. If your mind begins to wander, come back to your breath and the sensations occurring on the soles of your feet.

After you've completed your walk, stop and stand. Close your eyes and feel centered through your body and with the Earth. Feel the energy of the ground circulating through your body, restoring it and bringing your entire system into balance. Give gratitude to the Earth for supporting you as she has done your entire life. Also, thank yourself for taking this time to connect with nature.

You can practice this earthing and walking meditation at any time. You can even practice it in the rain to add new sensations and elements. Return to it anytime you feel drained, anxious, or disconnected from your intuition. This practice and Mother Earth are always available to support you on your journey.

VIRGO LUNAR FLOW

Virgo rules our digestive and nervous systems. The following sequence is designed to address these areas of your body by bringing fluidity to your energy and decreasing the nervous tension Virgo's energy often causes. You can practice this sequence throughout Virgo Season and on her New Moon. Please modify any poses for your body and vibration.

Begin by lying on your mat. Bring your awareness to your breath and count to 4 on the inhale and 4 on the exhale. Do this for 10 breaths before starting, and continue this equanimous breathing through the entire sequence.

SUPINE CRESCENT MOON POSE

While still lying down, stretch your arms overhead and bend your body to the right in the shape of a Crescent Moon, with both hips firmly on the ground. Lightly grab your left wrist and cross your right ankle over your left. Take 5 breaths here. Then switch sides for 5 breaths.

KNEE-TO-CHEST POSE

Still lying on the ground, hug your right knee into your chest and take 5 breaths. Switch sides for 5 breaths, then hug both knees into your body.

BOAT POSE

Still holding both knees into your chest, inhale and lift your nose to your knees. Then release your arms, extending them alongside your feet. On your exhale, stretch your legs outward for Boat Pose. On your next exhale, try to pike up to balancing on your sit bones in a V shape; you can bend your knees if needed. Take 5 breaths and release to a Cross-Seated Pose.

SEATED TWIST

From a crossed-legged position, exhale and twist to the right. Place your left hand on your right knee and your right hand behind you. On each inhale, expand through your chest and grow taller; on each exhale, twist a little more deeply. Continue for 5 breaths, then switch sides for another 5 breaths.

STANDING FORWARD BEND

Roll forward from a seated position to your feet and fold forward over your body. Allow your knees to bend slightly so your torso can rest on the top of your thighs. Catch the opposite elbows with your hands and relax here, lengthening through your spine, for 5 to 10 breaths. When finished, slowly roll up to standing.

SUN SALUTATION A

Start by standing on the top of your mat. Inhale and stretch your arms overhead. Exhale and fold forward. Inhale, lengthen out your back. Exhale, step back into Plank Pose and lower to the ground. Inhale, reach your chest up for Cobra Pose, legs staying on the ground. Exhale, stretch back to Downward Dog Pose. Stay here for 5 breaths and feel your entire body expand. On exhale, step back to the top of the mat. Inhale, lengthen out through your spine. Exhale, fold forward. Inhale, come up to standing, reaching your arms overhead. Exhale, return your hands to your heart. Pause for a moment and feel centered on the ground and through your body. Repeat this sequence three times.

Visit spiritdaughter.com/collections/zodiac-yoga to flow with our Virgo Zodiac Yoga video.

VIRGO LUNAR FLOW

WARRIOR 2 > REVERSE WARRIOR > TRIANGLE > WIDE-LEGGED FORWARD BEND

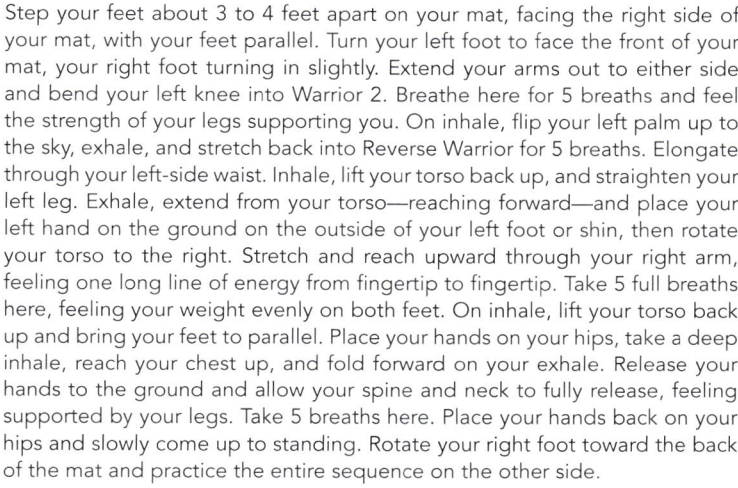

Step your feet about 3 to 4 feet apart on your mat, facing the right side of your mat, with your feet parallel. Turn your left foot to face the front of your mat, your right foot turning in slightly. Extend your arms out to either side and bend your left knee into Warrior 2. Breathe here for 5 breaths and feel the strength of your legs supporting you. On inhale, flip your left palm up to the sky, exhale, and stretch back into Reverse Warrior for 5 breaths. Elongate through your left-side waist. Inhale, lift your torso back up, and straighten your left leg. Exhale, extend from your torso—reaching forward—and place your left hand on the ground on the outside of your left foot or shin, then rotate your torso to the right. Stretch and reach upward through your right arm, feeling one long line of energy from fingertip to fingertip. Take 5 full breaths here, feeling your weight evenly on both feet. On inhale, lift your torso back up and bring your feet to parallel. Place your hands on your hips, take a deep inhale, reach your chest up, and fold forward on your exhale. Release your hands to the ground and allow your spine and neck to fully release, feeling supported by your legs. Take 5 breaths here. Place your hands back on your hips and slowly come up to standing. Rotate your right foot toward the back of the mat and practice the entire sequence on the other side.

CHAIR POSE > STANDING-FORWARD BEND

Return to the front of your mat. Keep your feet together and bend deeply into your knees as if you were sitting in a chair. Reach your arms upward to the sky and look up. Feel your belly drawing in, helping direct your tailbone to the floor. Breathe here for 5 breaths and feel the strength of your legs. Inhale, come back up to standing, exhale, and fold forward for 5 breaths, allowing your torso to lengthen again. On inhale, slowly roll up to standing.

ARDHA MATSYENDRASANA

Come to a seated position on your mat with your legs straight. Then bend your knees, placing your feet on the floor. Slide your right leg under your left one (which is still upright), placing your left foot by your right hip and laying your left leg on the ground. Tighten the pose by further crossing your left ankle over your right knee. Inhale, reach your left arm up to the sky, stretching your left-side waist. Exhale and twist to the right, either wrapping your arm around your left knee or hooking your right elbow around the side of your left leg with your palm facing left. Place your left hand behind yourself for support on the ground or on a block. Breathe here for 5 breaths, lengthening on each inhale and twisting deeper on each exhale.

BADDHA KONASANA

Come back to a neutral seated position and take the soles of your feet together, knees out to either side. Grab ahold of your feet and inhale as you lengthen through your spine. Exhale, fold over your legs, and breathe here for 5 to 10 minutes. Feel your inhales extend down into your hips, opening them, and your exhales relaxing your entire nervous system.

SAVASANA

Stretch both your legs out long on the mat and place your palms facing upward in a receptive position. Feel your entire body supported by the ground beneath you. Let your breath become natural and feel the energy circulating through you from your practice. Allow your mind to be still and your body to be calm.

VIRGO X THE NEW MOON

SEPTEMBER 14TH

The New Moon in Virgo brings details to our intentions. It reminds us that anything worth doing is worth doing well. Virgo teaches us to roll up our sleeves, dig in, and do the hard work needed to manifest the reality we want to live in. This New Moon holds the space for us to bring form to our visions. It's a time not only to see the path that leads to them but build it with our two hands. Virgo inspires us to make long-lasting commitments through our intentions. This is a night to see far into the future and feel it throughout your being. What do you want your life to look like in five or ten years? What can you do today to help you get there?

As you write your intentions this New Moon, feel into the power of your practices and rituals. The small things we do each day with intent become the rituals of our life. How you wake in the morning is a ritual. Having a pot of tea can be a ritual. Journaling is a ritual. These rituals become the foundation for your intentions to manifest. They keep the fire of your dreams burning long after the New Moon has passed and during even the most distracting times. Rituals also help us define our time. Virgo reminds us that our time is finite, and we must treat it as a precious resource. On this New Moon, feel into what rituals can help you slowly build your visions. Virgo reminds us that we are in a rush to reach our destination. The journey to our dreams is just as fulfilling as achieving them. What's important is that we create a strong foundation that will not waiver in the face of adversity.

As you create and commit to rituals that will help you work toward your visions, include rituals of healing. Virgo is one of the great healers of the zodiac. She reminds us that our wounds can sabotage us in ways we least expect. If we truly want a strong foundation, we must heal the cracks in our soul. When we have unprocessed grief or trauma from the past, it creates energetic noise in our system. It distracts us, takes us off course, and brings us out of the present moment. Our wounds can call in situations that repeat our past and cause chaos in our lives. Virgo is the sign of organization. She reminds us that to reach our highest visions, we must declutter our minds and hearts. As you form your intentions this New Moon, feel if any energies pull you back. Is there anything causing you doubt, telling

VIRGO X THE NEW MOON

SEPTEMBER 14TH

you that you are unworthy, or preventing you from believing you are capable of manifesting your visions? These feelings may be subtle, but notice if they come up. Address their root cause, and while you may not be able to heal them in one night, come up with a ritual to heal them over time.

Healing rituals look like daily journaling. They can be mantras you create to say when self-doubts arise. They may even be a plan when a certain thought or feeling comes up. This plan can include a breathing exercise, a series of questions to ask yourself, or a call to a loved one who can give you a different perspective. As you create various rituals for yourself this New Moon, include ones that build your intentions and ones that heal the piece of you that subconsciously tears down your intentions. Much of the work of manifestation is shifting what blocks you from receiving what is already yours.

ASPECTS

There are a few other astrological events happening on this New Moon. Mercury, Virgo's planetary ruler, is retrograde. When a planet is retrograde, it spins the energy inward. Mercury rules communications, making this New Moon a wonderful time to go inward and have a needed conversation with yourself. Ask yourself some of the more challenging questions this New Moon, and get to the bottom of any issues you have around self-worth or perfectionism. Now is the time to understand the root of these energies and communicate with the place within you that is attached to them.

It is important that you be crystal clear about your intentions before writing them on this New Moon. Mercury Retrograde can cause messages to become misinterpreted. If you are not clear, direct, and detailed in your intentions, then the Universe may not accurately hear them. You can never manifest the "wrong" energy, but you can send mixed signals to the Universe about what you really desire. If you write your intentions from a place of clarity, then there will be no room for misinterpretation. If you don't feel ready to write them, then wait a day or two until they are clear in your mind. Instead, spend time in meditation, practicing breath work, or working with other modalities that help you clear your mind and center your energy. Once you feel connected to your entire being, then write your intentions.

Helping ground your energy on this New Moon is a Grand Earth Trine between the Sun and Moon in Virgo, Uranus and Jupiter in Taurus, and Pluto in Capricorn. The abundance of Earth energy this day creates a container for your energy, helping settle your nervous system and bring clarity to your mind. Align deeply with the Earth today by walking in nature, holding an outdoor Moon circle, or meditating with a few plants. Feel the support of the Earth element helping to hold you and connect you to your body.

Also, feel this energy bringing clarity to your intentions. Earth represents the foundation we build everything else upon. Let this energy teach you about your foundation. What will help you manifest your visions? Think about routines, rituals, or practices that can serve as a reflection of the stable Earth in your life. Feel into what practices you can root into and draw nourishment and creativity from. Also, feel what practices can steady you when life becomes challenging or throws you curveballs. What brings you back to center again and again? Lean into the Earth element to help you feel what stabilizes you and connects you with your strength, resilience, and power.

SETTING UP FOR MAGIC

Each zodiac sign carries inherent energy. With this energy come colors, shapes, scents, and elements that match its vibration. For every New Moon, we want to incorporate as many of these frequencies as possible. While none of them is required to align with the energy of the New Moon, they do help reflect the energy. Think of them as energetic mirrors placed around the room to amplify and direct the energy. Use your intuition to guide the choice and placement of objects. Resist the urge to overthink where they belong. Let the crystals, in particular, choose their location; all you need to do is listen.

Pick a space that feels centered and stable, either inside or outside. Your circle should feel protected and safe. It also needs to be relatively quiet and free of distracting noises. For this Virgo New Moon, practice near the Earth if possible. If you can't practice outside, bring the Earth inside through flowers, plants, and crystals.

Once you designate a space for your circle, imagine a white light creating the boundary. Place a crystal, candle, or another piece of magic in the center to give structure to the circle. This center is also where you can set up a crystal grid to help further direct the energy. For Virgo, create a crystal grid in the shape of a star, hexagon, or pentagon. Earth crystal grids have a structured shape to them that helps bring grounding, order, and clarity to the space. If available, place a generator, or tower crystal, in the center. These crystals have six sides and amplify the other crystals in the grid.

If you are creating an altar, place it in the easterly corner to help call in the energy of new beginnings. You can adorn your altar with images that inspire new beginnings. You can also place images of your mentors and teachers, as the energy of mentorship belongs to Virgo and the Sixth House. You can also place on your altar flowers, crystals, jewelry, or other treasures that remind you of your journey, power, and potential. After you write your intentions, they can rest here as well.

After your altar and circle's center are in place, position other objects around the circle to anchor the four directions. You can also place magical items at key places in the circle, such as near the doorway for protection, or if a section feels energetically off in some way. You can use candles, crystals, flowers, plants, bowls of water, and anything else that feels special to you. Incorporate all the elements if possible, feeling supported in your work by all of them.

Know that your attention and awareness of the power available is the most important thing for working with it. You can practice the exercises in this workbook in any way you choose; you can practice alone, on a train, or in a group of people around a bonfire. Your willingness to open up, look within, and expand your consciousness is the most essential piece to this day.

The other pieces for calling in and aligning with the energy of Virgo are listed in the box to the right. You can combine them any way you like.

Once you've set up your circle, cleanse it through a purification ritual using a bundled dried herb like lavender or rosemary. Cleanse in the easternmost point of the circle and make your way around the circle in a clockwise direction. Know that as you cleanse the circle, you are also creating a container for the energy of the night. After the circle is cleansed, cleanse yourself and your friends before they enter the circle by waving the dried herb bundle from head to toe, encasing the whole body with smoke.

You can begin the circle by acknowledging everyone in the room. Have everyone introduce themselves and share their sign, their favorite flower, or some other piece of information that connects the circle. You can then continue to the yoga if you are practicing, and then the meditation. Once you feel the room is centered, talk

SETTING UP FOR MAGIC

FOR YOUR ALTAR OR MOON CIRCLE

FLOWERS:
Chrysanthemums, Ivy, Hyacinth,
+ Buttercups

COLORS:
Dark Greens, Tans, + Browns

TEXTURES/FABRIC:
Medium woods

SCENTS:
Rosemary, Lavender, + Sandalwood

SHAPES:
Rectangles + Hexagons

ELEMENTS:
Plants, Flowers

about the astrology of the night and what it means for each of you. If it is a larger circle, you may want to designate a talking stick or crystal that each guest holds while they speak.

After you've shared your understandings, continue with the questions and the journaling portion of this workbook. After everyone has finished, talk again about your experiences with the energy and the revelations that may have occurred. You can share as little or as much as you like with the group. Never feel obligated to speak; sometimes energies need time to develop before they are brought to the light of day. At this point, you may also pull some cards to help tune further into your intuitive guidance. You can use manifestation cards, oracle cards, tarot cards, goddess cards, animal medicine cards, or any other decks in your toolkit.

Once you've finished the circle, close it by having everyone shut their eyes and meditate on what they are grateful for that night and every night. You can even practice being grateful for things that haven't come your way yet. Gratitude will attract them to your energetic field and let the Universe know you are ready to receive them. Enjoy this time to be with your self, your heart, and your soul. Get to know yourself on a deeper level and allow your life to unfold another layer each New Moon.

your greatest mistakes can become
roadmaps for someone else's adventures.

-spirit daughter

NEW MOON QUESTIONS

These questions are designed to help you become clear in your intentions. Take a few deep breaths to ground yourself before answering them. Sit with each question for a moment and allow the answer to naturally arise, being open to the person you are becoming. As you write, know you are opening the door to your intuition and giving permission to your highest visions to come out and be seen.

1. What imperfections can you embrace with love and compassion?

_____

_____

_____

_____

_____

_____

_____

_____

_____

_____

2. What learning opportunity comes from your imperfections, mistakes, or faults?

_____

_____

_____

_____

_____

_____

_____

_____

_____

_____

3. What lessons have you learned that can be roadmaps for other people?

_____

_____

_____

_____

_____

_____

_____

_____

_____

_____

_____

_____

_____

4. What teachers, mentors, or guides are showing up in life to expand you?

_____

_____

_____

_____

_____

_____

_____

_____

_____

_____

_____

_____

_____

INTENTION SETTING

Setting intentions revolves around how you want to feel and what energy will help you create a life that nourishes those feelings. It is not about a to-do list of items you need to accomplish to encourage your dreams to manifest. It's about creating a vibration you can hold each month to help call in the support, guidance, healing, and intuition you need to make your visions a reality. Some intentions manifest overnight, while others take many Moons to come to fruition. It's important to be patient with yourself and this process. You may think you want one thing, but in reality, your higher Self knows better and will subtly direct you to the answers you need.

Before setting your intentions, make sure you are grounded in your body and connected to your breath. Feel your energy settle and be open to receiving guidance both from yourself and the Universe. Know this is your time to design your life. Feel your power to create your visions, and feel your strength. First, decide how you want to feel each day. Ask yourself what vibration you want to carry throughout your days and how this vibration reflects your joy. Hold space for the answers you seek to reveal themselves, and hold space for your feelings. Notice what emotions emerge when you begin to develop your visions. Do you feel worthy of your dreams? Do you feel good enough for them? Do you feel you deserve the life of your highest visions? If the answer to any of these questions is no, first uncover why before moving forward in your dreaming.

You can set your intentions within seventy-two hours of the New Moon exact, which occurs at 6:39 PM PT on September 14th. If you need more time to settle your energy or find more meaning in your emotions, give it to yourself. You do not need to feel that you have a timer on your intention-setting. You can work with these intentions all week if needed. The most important part is that you be clear on what you are asking for from yourself and the Universe. If you are not grounded in your energy, wait until you feel connected to yourself. You can also practice yoga, meditation, and breathwork as part of your intention-setting practice to help connect you with your deeper self.

Or the Virgo New Moon, it's most beneficial to create intentions around your gifts and unique offerings to the world. These intentions can include seeing your perfection and your worth. See yourself showing up fully in your power, giving your gifts to the world to help it heal and evolve. Include seeing yourself fully grounded and ready to take charge of your life. Also, envision developing healthy boundaries around your space and time, which allow for your self-care. Include different rituals, which will help you build your visions over time. Remember, with Virgo, it's a slow and steady course. Patience and commitment are key.

Take a moment and create a scene in your mind. In this scene, all that you wish to call in is already yours. All you desire to change has already occurred. Do not worry about how you will get there or the list of to-dos needed to accomplish your goals. Just focus on the feeling of already living your dream. Know with every ounce of your being that it is already true; it already exists for you. Also, know that your intuition, not your logic, will lead you to this dream.

Write in as much detail as possible, and write without limits. Just let your mind explore. Align with the energy of Virgo to clarify your dreams. What does your envisioned life fee like? How does this dream make you feel? What emotions does it bring up? As you write, feel a sense of gratitude for what you are dreaming; thank the Universe for giving it to you and thank yourself for creating it. Gratitude always creates abundance.

INTENTION SETTING

AFFIRMATIONS

The New Moon is a powerful day to dive inward to your most hidden subconscious thoughts and patterns. In this space, you'll find the programs that are directing your life behind the scenes, most of the time, without you even knowing. You can look to the house in which this New Moon falls for you to find some guidance on which area of your life these mantras might show up. For instance, if Virgo rules your Seventh House, look for programing around your relationships. What do you tell yourself about these things daily? Below, write down your old programming. These can be things like "I'll never be good enough" or "It's too hard," "I must try harder," or "I'm not capable." Then rewrite your old mantras into new ones that oppose and challenge the old ones. Repeat your new affirmations daily until the next New Moon. Repetition is the key to new programming.

PERSONAL SIGNS

VIRGO SUN

At their best, people with their Sun in Virgo are highly intuitive healers capable of great understanding and empathy. They live in service of others and find fulfillment in this role. They take great care to perfect their offering to the world and succeed once they learn to love themselves unconditionally.

Virgos have both the fortunate and unfortunate ability to see their greatness. They know their potential, and they set out arbitrary points to let them know if they are reaching that potential. Simply put, Virgos know how perfect life can be. This knowledge can do two things for Virgos: it can drive them mad as they try to achieve this unobtainable goal, or it can inspire them to focus on the journey and enjoy the climb to the top of a mountain they may never reach. The choice is theirs. Once they realize they will never obtain perfection, they become free to enjoy an imperfect life full of opportunity for growth. They start living and stop focusing on mistakes or regrets. Not all Virgos can reach this type of enlightenment. Those who do, though, empower themselves and others to live a life full of joy, healing, and evolution.

Virgos are powerful healers, both for themselves and others. They have a natural gift for knowing what needs to shift in someone's energy for them to feel whole once again. They possess an unparalleled skill of discernment and can quickly see the pieces of any puzzle. Where someone else may view an issue as a tangled web, Virgos can precisely pick apart the pieces and handle each one with grace and inner knowing. Once they learn to accept their gift, they can break down complex issues into bite-sized information others can digest. They also need to understand that their talents are good enough to give to others. Every Virgo needs to practice radical self-acceptance to increase their sense of worthiness to step into their true power.

Once a Virgo sees the beauty of their existence, they are ready to be of service and, more importantly, teach. Virgo is the sign of mentorship. They are the teachers of the world and have much to offer the collective. They see things others cannot understand. They also have a capacity for patience, which is a critical skill for any teacher. Virgos need to refine their patience through time in nature, where patience is expected. As they ground their energy and find their natural, unrushed rhythm, they can become the wise mentor they have always looked for but have never found. They become their own teacher.

VIRGO MOON

People with their Moon in Virgo need to feel needed. They enjoy being of service to others and go out of their way to help people reach their goals. They find genuine fulfillment when nourishing others. They also need to be appreciated for their efforts and often look for validation from others. While appreciation is a bond-building energy, Virgo Moons need to learn to appreciate themselves. They need to feel good enough and of value without anyone else telling them they are. This realization requires a lifetime of self-development and understanding.

Virgo Moons are best when they are working on themselves. They enjoy growth in all areas and energetically stagnate when not challenged. They are always trying to improve themselves, especially emotionally. They must be careful to not get caught up in perfectionism, and they must understand that growth is a journey, not a destination. They will always have more to learn and more to uncover. This is what makes life interesting and enjoyable.

Virgo

DISCERNMENT. PATIENCE. KIND-HEARTEDNESS. SERVICE.

In matters of the heart, Virgo Moons can be a bit emotionally detached. They are highly technical and discerning, and they can view love as an equation to solve instead of a magical journey of the heart. They need to find someone who pushes them out of their logical mind and encourages them to feel. Emotions can be uncomfortable for Virgo Moons because they always like to stay in control. But those emotions can also be freeing. Once a Virgo Moon finds the person who can open their heart, they have no trouble committing because this Earth sign loves stability.

ASTROLOGY FORECAST

AUGUST 23RD - SEPTEMBER 22ND

AUGUST 23: MERCURY RETROGRADE IN VIRGO

As the Sun enters Virgo, Mercury, also stations retrograde today. Mercury is Virgo's planetary ruler. This retrograde adds an interesting spin to the Virgo Sun Season. Virgo is detailed and direct. This energy thrives through organization that helps bring form to our intentions. Virgo likes routines, rituals, and experiences rooted in the physical plane.

Mercury adds the element of knowledge and mentorship to this sign. Virgo is knowledge-based, and this wisdom comes from intuition. It is felt, not thought. Mercury also rules Gemini. Its influence over Virgo, though, is quite different. Ruling Virgo, Mercury is more grounded and encourages mindful, often slower, action. It also illuminates the need for mentors and teachers. Part of the energy of Virgo teaches us that we are all students. No one in this world is perfect, and any imperfections are opportunities for growth. When we recognize our faults, we also recognize where we are in need of lessons and wisdom. Often, this acknowledgment causes us to seek mentors or knowledge from outside ourselves.

Acknowledging our imperfections also inspires us to teach others through our vulnerability. Our stories become our power, and when we accept our imperfections, we can also help others with theirs. The energy of Virgo takes on a very different tone when we view it through the lens of Mercury. We can see how our communication can teach, pass down wisdom, and even help heal the collective. We can also understand what knowledge we are looking for in this life and where we may find it.

ASTROLOGY FORECAST

AUGUST 23RD - SEPTEMBER 22ND

While Mercury is retrograde in Virgo, spend time contemplating your stories. This energy can bring a bit of chaos to the normally well-planned Virgo vibration. If you feel any disruptions in your life, look for the opportunity for better alignment. Allow some things to fall apart, with the trust that they will come back together stronger. Remember that Mercury Retrograde affords us a deeper look into our subconscious. We can have conversations with parts of ourselves that are normally hidden out of conscious view. As you work this transit over the next three weeks, challenge yourself to confront your fears around your imperfections. Look at your ability to accept your faults and see them as opportunities for growth. Here are a few tips for Mercury Retrograde in Virgo.

+ Spend time journaling about your imperfections. Where are you imperfect? Where do you have faults, and how do they show up in your world?

+ Look at your ability to grow through your imperfections. What are you open to learning that can help you accept yourself more or grow into a new version of yourself?

+ What lessons have emerged from "mistakes" or questionable choices you've made in your life? How can you see those events as learning opportunities and not mistakes? As you find the wisdom in your imperfections, is there anything you can teach others?

+ Finally, journal about what types of teachings or mentors you are ready for on your journey. Who can expand you beyond your imperfections? What wisdom do you feel capable of integrating into your energy right now?

+ Remember that these conversations are between you and yourself. You may wish to share them with a trusted mentor or friend, but make sure you have clarity on them first. Mercury Retrograde is notorious for miscommunication. Over this transit, be aware of who you are exchanging energy with and how. For the most part, keep your findings to yourself for now. There will be time to share them with others after Mercury stations direct on September 15.

AUGUST 24: FIRST QUARTER MOON IN SAGITTARIUS

This Virgo Season, we have two First Quarters in Sagittarius, a rare event. First Quarters help us build our intentions, and with Sagittarius theming these Moons, there is an opportunity for expansion. Sagittarius challenges Virgo's energy by asking us to let go of our habits and routines to find something more aligned with our soul. The squaring of these energies pulls our vibration in two directions. Part of us will want to stay with the familiar routines, while the other will earn for new experiences that break up our patterns.

This first First Quarter Moon in Sagittarius occurs at the beginning of Virgo Season. It inspires us to try something new that expands our reality and consciousness. We may end up creating a routine around this new thing, but the point is to do something different that takes you away from your attachments and into a new vibration. Sagittarius reminds us that everything we do is a journey and gives us valuable lessons, no matter their outcome. Where can you expand past your comfort zones and limiting beliefs to your next self?

ASTROLOGY FORECAST

AUGUST 23RD - SEPTEMBER 22ND

AUGUST 28: URANUS RETROGRADE IN TAURUS

Today, Uranus begins his annual backward motion. Known as the planet of change, Uranus shocks and awes with his eccentric ways. Traditionally the ruler of Aquarius, Uranus currently is stationed in Taurus, shaking the ground of our financial systems and environmental perspectives. Uranus breaks things up, and amongst the chaos, he brings us new ideas, new behaviors, and new normals. Uranus challenges us to see past the proverbial box and expand our consciousness beyond our conditioned patterns and limiting beliefs.

Over this transit, become more aware of how you react to change. Notice if you meet it with resistance or acceptance. Explore with a curious mind how you process shifts in your life. Also, notice if you feel like a victim of change or disempowered by it. How can you find new ways to empower yourself? How can you be the orchestrator of change and the visionary behind the shifts? This retrograde is a time to take action, and those actions can be huge ones with massive consequences for our lives and the lives of others. Uranus continually compels us to see new solutions to old problems. This energy teaches us to look at different angles and think beyond the imaginable. Yes, the changes we are experiencing may feel shocking, but how can you take that energy and direct it toward creating positive shifts in your life?

AUGUST 30: BLUE MOON IN PISCES

Please see the Pisces Full Moon Workbook

SEPTEMBER 3: VENUS DIRECT IN LEO

Venus ends its retrograde motion today in the sign of Leo. When planets station direct, their energy amplifies. Spend some time today feeling your heart. Make a list of what you've learned from your heart over the last six weeks of this retrograde. What messages have revealed themselves? Also recognize where you have healed your heart or are beginning to heal. Venus Retrograde is often the beginning or ending of healing. Perhaps you are finally finding closure to past pain, or maybe you are finally recognize where your heart needs more attention. Either way, recognize where you are on your journey of healing and be grateful for any revelations this retrograde brought you.

SEPTEMBER 4: JUPITER RETROGRADE IN TAURUS

Jupiter, the planet of luck and abundance, stations retrograde today until December 30. Jupiter expands us. It reminds us of our potential and capacity for growth. Jupiter is the largest planet and was almost a second Sun to our solar system. Its very nature exemplifies greatness and what happens when we don't reach for our full potential. Wherever Jupiter lies in your chart shows the area where you can experience the most growth in your life. It also can show where you stop short of shining your brightest out of fear or some other reason for keeping yourself small.

Jupiter wants you to reach the greatest version of yourself and wants you to shine. In retrograde, Jupiter asks you to look inward and realize that whatever greatness you are trying to manifest externally starts inside. We all have dreams and aspirations about what we want our lives to look like. We may have wishes of abundance or visions or success. We may even take steps to cultivate our visions and put plans in place to manifest them. However, Jupiter Retrograde reminds us that the biggest key to greatness is our own willingness to grow.

ASTROLOGY FORECAST

AUGUST 23RD - SEPTEMBER 22ND

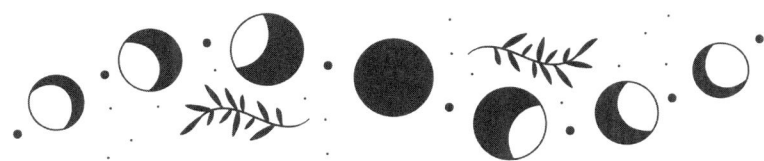

In Taurus, Jupiter expands our potential for abundance. Jupiter Retrograde, though, teaches us that abundance is an inside job. It does not happen because of something you do. It happens because of something you are. Same with any energy you are trying to manifest in your life. You have to do the work internally and become that energy before it becomes a dependable theme in your life. If you don't believe you are worthy of abundance, nothing you do will create it until you change that belief. Over this transit, focus on your self-worth and ask yourself if it is aligned with the abundance you desire. Do you believe you are worthy of your intentions? Do you believe the abundance is already yours? If any of these answers are no, you know where to focus this retrograde.

SEPTEMBER 6: LAST QUARTER IN GEMINI

Today we begin the final phase of this lunar cycle, the Last Quarter, which takes place in the energy of Gemini. It's a time to fearlessly question all the elements of your world. If the answers do not align with your vision and potential, then allow this waning Air Moon to sweep them away. Gemini is the energy of inspiration. It inspires us to be curious about everything. It also inspires us to be creative in our search for the truth.

When the Last Quarter is in Gemini, feel into your truths. Ask the hard questions about where you're going and how you're going to get there. Look over all the pieces of the puzzle that make up your life. Do they all fit? Look over the stories you tell yourself. Are they all true? Spend time with this energy as you survey your land and make changes where needed. Feel your heightened ability to make decisions today and use it to prepare yourself for the New Moon next week.

SEPTEMBER 22: FIRST QUARTER IN SAGITTARIUS (DOUBLE)

At the end of Virgo Season, we meet our second First Quarter Moon of the season. There are always challenges that pop up during this lunar phase. It's as if the Universe is testing us, and there is no right or wrong answer—only opportunities. With the Moon in Sagittarius and the Sun in Virgo, we are inspired to challenge our truths. We tend to tell ourselves so many stories, both negative and positive, out of sheer habit. Sagittarius asks us which are true and which need to be rewritten.

The First Quarter Moon is a time when our first blocks pop up around the intentions we set on the New Moon. Most of these barriers are internal, though, meaning we control them. As you work with both of these energies today, ask yourself how you can stay grounded while expanding the truths that govern your behavior. What tests are being handed to you, and how can they expand you? It's also a good time to remember that the tests from the Universe are also a way of asking you to show up and stand by your intentions to a stronger degree. Feel your unbreakable trust in your visions and their process of materialization today.

LIBRA SEASON

SEPTEMBER 22ND

Prepare to find harmony in your relationships and inner world, as we fall into the energy of balance and beauty with Libra Season.

PURCHASE AT SPIRITDAUGHTER.COM

HAPPY
NEW MOON!

Thank you to everyone who supported and purchased this workbook.

Special Thanks to Rebecca Reitz (rebeccareitz.com, @becca_reitz) for her beautiful artwork on the cover & pages 2, 4, 7, 8, 12, 16, 27, 28.

For a monthly subscription contact hello@spiritdaughter.com or visit www.spiritdaughter.com.

Disclaimer: The exercises and yoga sequences in this book are physical activities that should be performed carefully to avoid injury. You agree to accept all risks and release Spirit Daughter and any guest instructors from any and all liabilities. Please take care and enjoy.

Follow along our journey on IG:
@spiritdaughter

We always love seeing your photos & hearing about your experiences with the workbooks! Tag us to be featured on our community page:
@spiritdaughtercollective

We are
here to resonate
our particular essence
with the world - for the
world

Imagination
practice of Inner Sourcing
A way to Source the Soul
build our connection to our
Soul Self